KT-382-688

# POETRY
# FIRST AID
# KIT

POETRY FIRST AID KIT

Summersdale Publishers Ltd
46 West Street
Chichester
West Sussex
PO19 1RP
UK

www.summersdale.com

Printed and bound by CPI Group (UK) Ltd, Croydon, CR0 4YY

ISBN: 978-1-84953-465-9

Substantial discounts on bulk quantities of Summersdale books are available to corporations, professional associations and other organisations. For details contact Nicky Douglas by telephone: +44 (0) 1243 756902, fax: +44 (0) 1243 786300 or email: nicky@summersdale.com.

# POETRY
# FIRST AID
# KIT

Poems for Everyday Dilemmas,
Decisions and Emergencies

## ABBIE HEADON

summersdale

# CONTENTS

# INTRODUCTION

Although many of us can remember staring listlessly out of the classroom window while a teacher tried to inform us about sonnet form, or iambic pentameters, I think it's equally true that for everyone there's a poem, or even just a line or two of poetry, that rings pleasantly in the mind's ear and lingers in the memory (to borrow a phrase from a well-known poem). If you doubt it, just take a look at these and see if they don't stir something within you:

> *If you can keep your head when all about you*
> *Are losing theirs and blaming it on you...*

> *Once more unto the breach,*
> *dear friends, once more!*

> *No man is an island,*
> *Entire of itself.*

It seems that a few well-chosen words, arranged rhythmically and with that strange tension between ideas that are easy to understand and ones that stretch our definitions of the world we live in, can lodge themselves in our memories, ready to pop up unbidden in times of need or simply when a particular word arises in conversation.

My aim with the *Poetry First Aid Kit* has been to assemble a selection of verses that will soothe a perplexed mind in times of difficulty, from situations both deeply serious and all too mundane. Within these pages you will find lines to assist in all sorts of situations, from the schoolroom to the office, from the first sparks of romance to the mellower moments of married life, from business strategies to beauty concerns.

Some poems in this collection were aimed originally at one particular gender, but I believe that the wisdom they contain may apply to anyone. So, when Sir John Suckling advises an unsuccessful suitor that, 'If of herself she will not love, / Nothing can make her: / The devil take her!', I hope that lovers of any gender facing endless obduracy from their beloved may take comfort from his blunt advice.

The book is organised into thematic chapters, to guide readers to the poems that will be of most assistance in specific crises. However, it may be just as pleasurable and restorative to dive into the book at random, or read it from cover to cover, as poetry is a broad and mysterious art form, and who knows where its counsel may lead you...

Whether you're reeling from one of life's blows or simply searching for inspiration, I hope the *Poetry First Aid Kit* will provide enlightenment, comfort and a smile or two.

Abbie Headon, 2013

# EVERYDAY LIFE

# If you have a rodent problem that you don't want to deal with:

## Anarchism

Rats undermined the wall,
And while men slept
The floods that basined in the hills, smiled at the day,
Crept in by stealth and tore their bounds away:
And onward swept
Where busy towns in tranquil beauty kept
The peace; and with the power of many waters pent
Homes were engulfed and hills in twain were rent.
Steeple and tower
Fell toppling down, and in a breath
Where happiness had dwelt, were devastation,
woe and death,
And these few words were written of the fall:
While watchman slept
Rats undermined the wall.

**Albert Annett (1861–1936)**

# If a heavy grey sky is making you feel depressed:

# *from* The Cloud

I bring fresh showers for the thirsting flowers,
From the seas and the streams;
I bear light shade for the leaves when laid
In their noonday dreams.
From my wings are shaken the dews that waken
The sweet buds every one,
When rocked to rest on their mother's breast,
As she dances about the sun.
I wield the flail of the lashing hail,
And whiten the green plains under,
And then again I dissolve it in rain,
And laugh as I pass in thunder.

**Percy Bysshe Shelley (1792–1822)**

**If you think it could be interesting to sleepwalk but have never experienced it:**

## The Imaginative Crisis

Oh, solitude! thou wonder-working fay,
Come nurse my feeble fancy in your arms,
Though I, and thee, and fancy town-pent lay,
Come, call around, a world of country charms.
Let all this room, these walls dissolve away,
And bring me Surrey's fields to take their place:
This floor be grass, and draughts as breezes play;
Yon curtains trees, to wave in summer's face;
My ceiling, sky; my water-jug a stream;
My bed, a bank, on which to muse and dream.
The spell is wrought: imagination swells
My sleeping-room to hills, and woods, and dells!
I walk abroad, for naught my footsteps hinder,
And fling my arms. Oh! mi! I've broke the WINDER!

**Anonymous**

## If you have dropped your aunt's best willow-pattern plate:

## The Broken Dish

What's life but full of care and doubt
With all its fine humanities,
With parasols we walk about,
Long pigtails, and such vanities.

We plant pomegranate trees and things,
And go in gardens sporting,
With toys and fans of peacocks' wings,
To painted ladies courting.

We gather flowers of every hue,
And fish in boats for fishes,
Build summer-houses painted blue, –
But life's as frail as dishes!
Walking about their groves of trees,
Blue bridges and blue rivers,
How little thought them two Chinese,
They'd both be smashed to shivers!

**Thomas Hood (1799–1845)**

## If mowing the lawn seems a tedious task, bereft of inspiration:

## *from* Leaves of Grass

A child said *What is the grass?*
fetching it to me with full hands;
How could I answer the child?
I do not know what it is any more than he.

I guess it must be the flag of my disposition,
out of hopeful green stuff woven.

Or I guess it is the handkerchief of the Lord,
A scented gift and remembrancer designedly dropt,
Bearing the owner's name someway in the corners,
that we may see and remark, and say *Whose?*

Or I guess the grass is itself a child, the produced
babe of the vegetation.

Or I guess it is a uniform hieroglyphic,
And it means, Sprouting alike in broad zones and
narrow zones,
Growing among black folks as among white,
Kanuck, Tuckahoe, Congressman, Cuff, I give them
the same, I receive them the same.

And now it seems to me the beautiful uncut hair
of graves.

**Walt Whitman (1819–1892)**

**If you need to ask for a green-fingered friend's help with your garden (again):**

## Sent with a Flower Pot, Begging a Slip of Geranium

I've sent my empty pot again,
To beg another slip;
The last you gave, I'm griev'd to tell,
December's frost did nip.

I love fair Flora and her train,
But nurse her children ill;
I tend too little or too much;
They die from want of skill.

I blush to trouble you again,
Who've serv'd me oft before;
But, should this die, I'll break the pot,
And trouble you no more.

**Christian Milne (1773–1816)**

# If you need a new perspective on this evening's cooking:

## Anglo-Saxon Riddle

I'm a strange creature, for I satisfy women,
a service to the neighbours! No one suffers
at my hands except for my slayer.
I grow tall, erect in a bed,
I'm hairy underneath. From time to time
a good-looking girl, the doughty daughter
of some churl dares to hold me,
grips my russet skin, robs me of my head
and puts me in the pantry. At once that girl
with plaited hair who has confined me
remembers our meeting. Her eye moistens.

**Anonymous**

**If any so-called 'pillars of society' turn out not to be so exalted and worthy after all:**

## Ozymandias

I met a traveller from an antique land
Who said: Two vast and trunkless legs of stone
Stand in the desert. Near them, on the sand,
Half sunk, a shattered visage lies, whose frown,
And wrinkled lip, and sneer of cold command,
Tell that its sculptor well those passions read
Which yet survive, stamped on these lifeless things,
The hand that mocked them and the heart that fed:
And on the pedestal these words appear:
'My name is Ozymandias, king of kings:
Look on my works, ye Mighty, and despair!'
Nothing beside remains. Round the decay
Of that colossal wreck, boundless and bare
The lone and level sands stretch far away.

**Percy Bysshe Shelley (1792–1822)**

## If you want to splash out on something beautiful but aren't sure whether you should:

## *from* Endymion

A thing of beauty is a joy for ever:
Its loveliness increases; it will never
Pass into nothingness; but still will keep
A bower quiet for us, and a sleep
Full of sweet dreams, and health, and quiet breathing.
Therefore, on every morrow, are we wreathing
A flowery band to bind us to the earth,
Spite of despondence, of the inhuman dearth
Of noble natures, of the gloomy days,
Of all the unhealthy and o'er-darkened ways
Made for our searching: yes, in spite of all,
Some shape of beauty moves away the pall
From our dark spirits.

**John Keats (1795–1821)**

# CHILDHOOD
# AND YOUTH

**If adults can't understand why you need to play and make a rumpus:**

# The Children and Sir Nameless

Sir Nameless, once of Athelhall, declared:
'These wretched children romping in my park
Trample the herbage till the soil is bared,
And yap and yell from early morn till dark!
Go keep them harnessed to their set routines:
Thank God I've none to hasten my decay;
For green remembrance there are better means
Than offspring, who but wish their sires away.'

Sir Nameless of that mansion said anon:
'To be perpetuate for my mightiness
Sculpture must image me when I am gone.'
– He forthwith summoned carvers there express
To shape a figure stretching seven-odd feet
(For he was tall) in alabaster stone,
With shield, and crest, and casque, and sword complete:
When done a statelier work was never known.

Three hundred years hied; Church-restorers came,
And, no one of his lineage being traced,
They thought an effigy so large in frame
Best fitted for the floor. There it was placed,
Under the seats for schoolchildren. And they
Kicked out his name, and hobnailed off his nose;
And, as they yawn through sermon-time, they say,
'Who was this old stone man beneath our toes?'

**Thomas Hardy (1840–1928)**

**If sitting in front of the television seems more appealing than going to the park:**

## The Swing

How do you like to go up in a swing,
Up in the air so blue?
Oh, I do think it the pleasantest thing
Ever a child can do!

Up in the air and over the wall,
Till I can see so wide,
Rivers and trees and cattle and all
Over the countryside –

Till I look down on the garden green,
Down on the roof so brown –
Up in the air I go flying again,
Up in the air and down!

**Robert Louis Stevenson (1850–1894)**

**If you are wondering which is the best musical instrument to learn:**

## *from* Song for St Cecilia's Day

The trumpet's loud clangour
Excites us to arms,
With shrill notes of anger,
And mortal alarms.
The double double double beat
Of the thundering drum
Cries Hark! the foes come;
Charge, charge, 'tis too late to retreat!

The soft complaining flute,
In dying notes, discovers
The woes of hopeless lovers,
Whose dirge is whisper'd by the warbling lute.
Sharp violins proclaim
Their jealous pangs and desperation,
Fury, frantic indignation,
Depth of pains, and height of passion,
For the fair, disdainful dame.

**John Dryden (1631–1700)**

## If a rainy day forces you to play indoors:

# Block City

What are you able to build with your blocks?
Castles and palaces, temples and docks.
Rain may keep raining, and others go roam,
But I can be happy and building at home.

Let the sofa be mountains, the carpet be sea,
There I'll establish a city for me:
A kirk and a mill and a palace beside,
And a harbour as well where my vessels may ride.

Great is the palace with pillar and wall,
A sort of a tower on the top of it all,
And steps coming down in an orderly way
To where my toy vessels lie safe in the bay.

This one is sailing and that one is moored:
Hark to the song of the sailors on board!
And see on the steps of my palace, the kings
Coming and going with presents and things!

Now I have done with it, down let it go!
All in a moment the town is laid low.
Block upon block lying scattered and free,
What is there left of my town by the sea?

Yet as I saw it, I see it again,
The kirk and the palace, the ships and the men,
And as long as I live and where'er I may be,
I'll always remember my town by the sea.

**Robert Louis Stevenson (1850–1894)**

## If you are sick of being told to 'grow up':

# *from* Though Some Say That Youth Rules Me

Though some say that youth rules me,
I trust in age to tarry.
God and my right, and my duty,
From them shall I never vary,
Though some say that youth rules me.

I pray you all that aged be
How well did you your youth carry?
I think some worse of each degree.
Therein a wager lay dare I,
Though some say that youth rules me.

Pastimes of youth some time among
None can say but necessary.
I hurt no man, I do no wrong,
I love true where I did marry,
Though some say that youth rules me.

**King Henry VIII (1491–1547)**

## If you are both nervous and excited about a new challenge:

# I Stepped from Plank to Plank

I stepped from plank to plank
So slow and cautiously;
The stars about my head I felt,
About my feet the sea.

I knew not but the next
Would be my final inch, –
This gave me that precarious gait
Some call experience.

**Emily Dickinson (1830–1886)**

## If going to bed seems too utterly boring:

# My Bed is a Boat

My bed is like a little boat;
Nurse helps me in when I embark;
She girds me in my sailor's coat
And starts me in the dark.

At night I go on board and say
Good-night to all my friends on shore;
I shut my eyes and sail away
And see and hear no more.

And sometimes things to bed I take,
As prudent sailors have to do;
Perhaps a slice of wedding-cake,
Perhaps a toy or two.

All night across the dark we steer;
But when the day returns at last,
Safe in my room beside the pier,
I find my vessel fast.

**Robert Louis Stevenson (1850–1894)**

# STUDENT DAYS

## If you are wondering whether to study or be with your lover:

## *from* To Fanny

... for you to be buried in books –
Oh, Fanny! they're pitiful sages;
Who could not in one of your looks
Read more than in millions of pages!

Astronomy finds in your eyes
Better light than she studies above,
And Music must borrow your sighs
As the melody fittest for Love.

In Ethics – 't is you that can check,
In a minute, their doubts and their quarrels;
Oh! show but that mole on your neck,
And 't will soon put an end to their morals.

Your Arithmetic only can trip
When to kiss and to count you endeavor;
But eloquence glows on your lip
When you swear that you'll love me forever.

Thus you see what a brilliant alliance
Of arts is assembled in you, –
A course of more exquisite science
Man need never wish to pursue.

And, oh! – if a Fellow like me
May confer a diploma of hearts,
With my lip thus I seal your degree,
My divine little Mistress of Arts!

**Thomas Moore (1779–1852)**

# If you need help choosing a career:

# What will be your Profession?

**[Choose a number from 1 to 28 before you begin.]**

1. A *Lawyer* you are like to be,
And plead the cause of misery.

2. A *Farmer*, you will walk your fields,
Enjoying all your planting yields.

3. You a *Physician* good will make,
And physic rather give than take.

4. A *Sailor*'s watch perchance you'll keep,
And rock upon the ocean deep.

5. A *Clergyman* you yet may be,
From worldly strife and passion free.

14. Behind the *Counter* you will stand,
And serve the ladies of the land.

15. An *Architect*. Your fate will be
To raise up buildings fair to see.

16. A *Blacksmith*'s toil will be your aim,
And on the anvil rests your fame.

17. Keeping a large hotel you'll live,
And many an entertainment give.

18. To you it may seem very strange,
But you a *Pedlar* round will range.

19. *Professor* in a college, you
Will find hard work enough to do.

20. *Sawing wood* seems not the thing,
But down to that your pride you'll bring.

21. A *Senator* of high renown,
Your name will go to ages down.

22. I think that you will keep a *Store*;
The Fates say neither less nor more.

23. The strangest thing that has been said,
Is that a *Crown* will grace your head.

24. In legislative halls you'll stand,
Among the favourites of the land.

25. A *Miller*, not a Millerite,
You will wear a dress of white.

26. Over a college you will be
*President*, of high degree.

27. Your mind will be at constant strife,
To choose your pathway into life.

28. An *Author*'s wreath will deck your name,
And you will gather praise and fame.

**Caroline Gilman (1794–1888)**

## If you have been labelled an 'eternal student':

## *from* An Essay On Criticism

A little learning is a dangerous thing;
Drink deep, or taste not the Pierian spring:
There shallow draughts intoxicate the brain,
And drinking largely sobers us again.
Fired at first sight with what the Muse imparts,
In fearless youth we tempt the heights of Arts;
While from the bounded level of our mind
Short views we take, nor see the lengths behind,
But, more advanced, behold with strange surprise
New distant scenes of endless science rise!
So pleased at first the towering Alps we try,
Mount o'er the vales, and seem to tread the sky;
The eternal snows appear already past,
And the first clouds and mountains seem the last;
But those attained, we tremble to survey
The growing labours of the lengthened way;
The increasing prospect tires our wandering eyes,
Hill peep o'er hills, and Alps on Alps arise!

**Alexander Pope (1688–1744)**

# THE LIFE
# ARTISTIC

# If you have written a book but worry that people won't like it:

## *Ad librum suum*

My little book: who will thou please, tell me?
All which shall read thee? No that cannot be.
Whom then, the best? But few of these are known.
How shall thou know to please, thou know'st not whom?
The meaner sort commend not poetry;
And sure the worst should please themselves for thee:
But let them pass, and set by most no store,
Please thou one well, thou shall not need please more.

**Thomas Bastard (1566–1618)**

**If you have been accused of reading too much:**

# To a Lady, Who Said It Was Sinful to Read Novels

To love these Books, and harmless Tea,
Has always been my foible,
Yet will I ne'er forgetful be
To read my Psalms and Bible.

Travels I like, and Hist'ry too,
Or entertaining Fiction;
Novels and Plays I'd have a few,
If sense and proper diction.

I love a natural harmless Song,
But I cannot sing like Handel;
Depriv'd of such resource, the tongue
Is sure employ'd – in scandal.

**Christian Milne (1773–1816)**

# If dreams of fame are preoccupying you:

## *from* An Essay on Man

What's fame? a fancy'd life in others' breath,
A thing beyond us, ev'n before our death.
Just what you hear, you have, and what's unknown
The same (my lord) if Tully's, or your own.
All that we feel of it begins and ends
In the small circle of our foes or friends;
To all beside as much an empty shade
An Eugene living, as a Caesar dead;
Alike or when, or where, they shone, or shine,
Or on the Rubicon, or on the Rhine.
A wit's a feather, and a chief a rod;
An honest man's the noblest work of God.
Fame but from death a villain's name can save,
As justice tears his body from the grave;
When what t' oblivion better were resign'd,
Is hung on high, to poison half mankind.

All fame is foreign, but of true desert;
Plays round the head, but comes not to the heart:
One self-approving hour whole years out-weighs
Of stupid starers, and of loud huzzas;
And more true joy Marcellus exil'd feels,
Than Caesar with a senate at his heels.

**Alexander Pope (1688–1744)**

**If you despair of ever being able to describe true beauty in words:**

# He Tells of the Perfect Beauty

O cloud-pale eyelids, dream-dimmed eyes,
The poets labouring all their days
To build a perfect beauty in rhyme
Are overthrown by a woman's gaze
And by the unlabouring brood of the skies:
And therefore my heart will bow, when dew
Is dropping sleep, until God burn time,
Before the unlabouring stars and you.

**William Butler Yeats (1865–1939)**

## If you are mocked for loving Shakespeare and his works:

# Shakespeare

Others abide our question. Thou art free.
We ask and ask: Thou smilest and art still,
Out-topping knowledge. For the loftiest hill
That to the stars uncrowns his majesty,
Planting his steadfast footsteps in the sea,
Making the heaven of heavens his dwelling-place,
Spares but the cloudy border of his base
To the foil'd searching of mortality;
And thou, who didst the stars and sunbeams know,
Self-school'd, self-scann'd, self-honour'd, self-secure,
Didst walk on earth unguess'd at. Better so!
All pains the immortal spirit must endure,
All weakness that impairs, all griefs that bow,
Find their sole voice in that victorious brow.

**Matthew Arnold (1822–1888)**

# If people say your taste in music is strange:

# To Music

Here's to Music,
Joy of joys!
One man's music's
Another man's noise.

**Oliver Herford (1863–1935)**

**If you have been accused of being a dreamer, with your head in the clouds:**

## *from* My Mind to Me a Kingdom Is

My mind to me a kingdom is;
Such present joys therein I find,
That it excels all other bliss
That earth affords or grows by kind:
Though much I want that most would have,
Yet still my mind forbids to crave.

[...]

Content I live, this is my stay;
I seek no more than may suffice;
I press to bear no haughty sway;
Look, what I lack my mind supplies.
Lo, thus I triumph like a king,
Content with that my mind doth bring.

**Sir Edward Dyer (1543–1607)**

## If people tell you that the arts are not as important as 'real' work:

## *from* Ode

We are the music-makers,
And we are the dreamers of dreams,
Wandering by lone sea-breakers,
And sitting by desolate streams;
World-losers and world-forsakers,
On whom the pale moon gleams;
Yet we are the movers and shakers
Of the world for ever, it seems.

With wonderful deathless ditties
And out of a fabulous story
We build up the world's great cities,
We fashion an empire's glory;
One man with a dream, at pleasure,
Shall go forth and conquer a crown;
And three with a new song's measure
Can trample an empire down.

We, in the ages lying
In the buried past of the earth,
Built Nineveh with our sighing,
And Babel itself with our mirth;
And o'erthrew them with prophesying
To the old of the new world's worth;
For each age is a dream that is dying,
Or one that is coming to birth.

**Arthur O'Shaughnessy (1844–1881)**

# BEAUTY AND APPEARANCE

# If you worry that you are not tall enough:

# It Is Not Growing Like a Tree

It is not growing like a tree
In bulk doth make Man better be;
Or standing long an oak, three hundred year,
To fall a log at last, dry, bald, and sere:
A lily of a day
Is fairer far in May,
Although it fall and die that night;
It was the plant and flower of light.
In small proportions we just beauties see;
And in short measures life may perfect be.

**Ben Jonson (1572–1637)**

# If you worry about your freckles:

## Pied Beauty

Glory be to God for dappled things –
For skies of couple-colour as a brinded cow;
For rose-moles all in stipple upon trout that swim;
Fresh-firecoal chestnut-falls; finches' wings;
Landscape plotted and pieced – fold, fallow, and plough;
And áll trádes, their gear and tackle and trim.

All things counter, original, spare, strange;
Whatever is fickle, freckled (who knows how?)
With swift, slow; sweet, sour; adazzle, dim;
He fathers-forth whose beauty is past change:
Praise him.

**Gerard Manley Hopkins (1844–1889)**

**If it drives you crazy when people say,
'You've got your mother's eyes':**

# Heredity

I am the family face;
Flesh perishes, I live on,
Projecting trait and trace
Through time to times anon,
And leaping from place to place
Over oblivion.

The years-heired feature that can
In curve and voice and eye
Despise the human span
Of durance – that is I;
The eternal thing in man,
That heeds no call to die.

**Thomas Hardy (1840–1928)**

**If you are worried that you aren't dressed smartly enough for a first date:**

## Delight in Disorder

A sweet disorder in the dress
Kindles in clothes a wantonness:
A lawn about the shoulders thrown
Into a fine distraction:
An erring lace which here and there
Enthrals the crimson stomacher:
A cuff neglectful, and thereby
Ribbons to flow confusedly:
A winning wave (deserving note)
In the tempestuous petticoat:
A careless shoe-string, in whose tie
I see a wild civility:
Do more bewitch me than when art
Is too precise in every part.

**Robert Herrick (1591–1674)**

# If the world of fashion is baffling to you:

## The Feather Boa

This animal of which I speak
Is a most curious sort of freak.
Though Serpent would its form describe,
Yet it is of the feathered tribe.
And 'tis the snake, I do believe,
That tempted poor old Mother Eve,
For never woman did exist
Who could its subtle charm resist.

**Carolyn Wells (1862–1942)**

# ROMANCE

**If you are madly in love and others say you should be more cautious:**

## Sonnet from the Portuguese XLIII

How do I love thee? Let me count the ways.
I love thee to the depth and breadth and height
My soul can reach, when feeling out of sight
For the ends of Being and ideal Grace.
I love thee to the level of everyday's
Most quiet need, by sun and candlelight.
I love thee freely, as men strive for Right;
I love thee purely, as they turn from Praise.
I love thee with the passion put to use
In my old griefs, and with my childhood's faith.
I love thee with a love I seemed to lose
With my lost saints, – I love thee with the breath,
Smiles, tears, of all my life! – and, if God choose,
I shall but love thee better after death.

**Elizabeth Barrett Browning (1806–1861)**

## If you are wondering whether to send an email or a handwritten love letter:

# Sonnet 65

Since brass, nor stone, nor earth, nor boundless sea,
But sad mortality o'ersways their power,
How with this rage shall beauty hold a plea,
Whose action is no stronger than a flower?
O how shall summer's honey breath hold out
Against the wreckful siege of battering days,
When rocks impregnable are not so stout
Nor gates of steel so strong, but Time decays?
O fearful meditation! where, alack,
Shall Time's best jewel from Time's chest lie hid?
Or what strong hand can hold his swift foot back,
Or who his spoil of beauty can forbid?
O! none, unless this miracle have might,
That in black ink my love may still shine bright.

**William Shakespeare (1564–1616)**

## If you can't find the exact words you need to express your love:

## Expression

A hackneyed burden, to a hackneyed air,
'I love thee only, thou art wondrous fair!'
Alas! the poets have worn the theme threadbare!

Can I not find some words less tame and old,
To paint thy form and face of perfect mould,
Thy dewy lips, thy hair of brown and gold?

Can I not sing in somewhat fresher strain
The love I lavish and receive again,
The thrilling joy, so like to thrilling pain?

Can I not, by some metaphor divine,
Describe the life I quaff like nectared wine
In being thine, and knowing thou art mine?

Ah, no! this halting verse can naught express;
No English words can half the truth confess,
That have not all been rhymed to weariness!

So let me cease my scribbling for to-day,
And maiden, turn thy lovely face this way,
Words will not do, but haply kisses may!

**George Arnold (1834–1865)**

**If you are considering playing hard to get:**

# A Youth for Jane with Ardour Sighed

A youth for Jane with ardour sighed,
  The maid with sparkling eye;
But to his vows she still replied,
  'I'll hear you by and by.'

'Suspense (he cries) my bloom decays,
  And bids my spirits fly;
Now hear my vows,' – but still she says,
  'I'll hear you by and by.'

At length her frowns his love subdue,
  He shuns her scornful eye,
And Emma seeks, who'll hear him woo
  Both now, and by and by.

And soon to church he leads the maid,
When lo! he sees draw nigh,
The now repentant fair who said
She'd hear him by and by.

'Hear me (she cries): no more in vain
Thy heart for me shall sigh!' –
'I'm busy now (said he) – but, Jane!
I'll hear you by and by.'

**Amelia Opie (1769–1853)**

## If a biting insect is spoiling your romantic tête-à-tête:

## The Flea

Mark but this flea, and mark in this,
How little that which thou deniest me is;
It suck'd me first, and now sucks thee,
And in this flea our two bloods mingled be.
Thou know'st that this cannot be said
A sin, nor shame, nor loss of maidenhead;
Yet this enjoys before it woo,
And pamper'd swells with one blood made of two;
And this, alas! is more than we would do.

O stay, three lives in one flea spare,
Where we almost, yea, more than married are.
This flea is you and I, and this
Our marriage bed, and marriage temple is.
Though parents grudge, and you, we're met,
And cloister'd in these living walls of jet.
Though use make you apt to kill me,
Let not to that self-murder added be,
And sacrilege, three sins in killing three.

Cruel and sudden, hast thou since
Purpled thy nail in blood of innocence?
Wherein could this flea guilty be,
Except in that drop which it suck'd from thee?
Yet thou triumph'st, and say'st that thou
Find'st not thyself nor me the weaker now.
'Tis true; then learn how false fears be;
Just so much honour, when thou yield'st to me,
Will waste, as this flea's death took life from thee.

**John Donne (1572–1631)**

## If you are thinking of serenading your lover on a cold winter's night:

# Fatal Love

Poor Hal caught his death standing under a spout
Expecting till midnight when Nan would come out;
But fatal his patience, as cruel the dame,
And cursed was the weather that
quench'd the man's flame.
Whoe'er thou art that reads these moral lines,
Make love at home, and go to bed betimes.

**Matthew Prior (1664–1721)**

**If your beloved thinks it's silly to write your names on a sandy beach:**

## One Day I Wrote Her Name Upon the Strand

One day I wrote her name upon the strand,
But came the waves and washèd it away:
Again I wrote it with a second hand,
But came the tide and made my pains his prey.
Vain man (said she) that dost in vain assay
A mortal thing so to immortalise;
For I myself shall like to this decay,
And eke my name be wipèd out likewise.
Not so (quod I); let baser things devise
To die in dust, but you shall live by fame;
My verse your virtues rare shall eternise,
And in the heavens write your glorious name:
Where, when as Death shall all the world subdue,
Our love shall live, and later life renew.

**Edmund Spenser (1552–1599)**

**If your lover cannot afford expensive presents, but can only give you their love:**

## He Wishes for the Cloths of Heaven

Had I the heavens' embroidered cloths,
Enwrought with golden and silver light,
The blue and the dim and the dark cloths
Of night and light and the half-light,
I would spread the cloths under your feet:
But I, being poor, have only my dreams;
I have spread my dreams under your feet;
Tread softly because you tread on my dreams.

**William Butler Yeats (1865–1939)**

# LOVE'S CHALLENGES

**If you love somebody, but struggle to speak your feelings aloud:**

## Astrophel and Stella, Sonnet 54

Because I breathe not love to every one,
Nor do not use set colours for to wear,
Nor nourish special locks of vowed hair,
Nor give each speech the full point of a groan,
The courtly nymphs, acquainted with the moan
Of them, who in their lips Love's standard bear;
'What he?' say they of me. 'Now I dare swear,
He cannot love. No, no, let him alone.'
And think so still, so Stella know my mind,
Profess indeed I do not Cupid's art;
But you, fair maids, at length this true shall find:
That his right badge is worn but in the heart;
Dumb swans, not chatt'ring pies, do lovers prove;
They love indeed, who quake to say they love.

**Sir Philip Sidney (1554–1586)**

## If you have a severe case of unrequited love:

# Why so Pale and Wan?

Why so pale and wan, fond lover?
Prithee, why so pale?
Will, when looking well can't move her,
Looking ill prevail?
Prithee, why so pale?

Why so dull and mute, young sinner?
Prithee, why so mute?
Will, when speaking well can't win her,
Saying nothing do 't?
Prithee, why so mute?

Quit, quit for shame! This will not move;
This cannot take her.
If of herself she will not love,
Nothing can make her:
The devil take her!

**Sir John Suckling (1609–1642)**

**If you have waited for love so long that you have almost given up hope:**

## *from* Love Will Find Out the Way

Over the mountains
And over the waves,
Under the fountains
And under the graves;
Under floods that are deepest,
Which Neptune obey,
Over rocks that are steepest,
Love will find out the way.

When there is no place
For the glow-worm to lie,
When there is no space
For receipt of a fly;
When the midge dares not venture
Lest herself fast she lay,
If Love come, he will enter
And will find out the way.

**Anonymous**

## If you and your lover are clinging together through difficult times:

## *from* Love is Enough

Love is enough: though the World be a-waning,
And the woods have no voice but the voice of complaining,
Though the sky be too dark for dim eyes to discover
The gold-cups and daisies fair blooming thereunder,
Though the hills be held shadows, and the sea a dark wonder,
And this day draw a veil over all deeds pass'd over,
Yet their hands shall not tremble, their feet shall not falter;
The void shall not weary, the fear shall not alter
These lips and these eyes of the loved and the lover.

**William Morris (1834–1896)**

# If you are missing a distant lover:

## Absence, Hear Thou My Protestation

Absence, hear thou my protestation
Against thy strength,
Distance and length:
Do what thou canst for alteration;
For hearts of truest mettle
Absence doth join, and time doth settle.

Who loves a mistress of such quality,
He soon hath found
Affection's ground
Beyond time, place, and all mortality.
To hearts that cannot vary
Absence is present, time doth tarry.

My senses want their outward motions,
Which now within
Reason doth win
Redoubl'd in her secret notions;
Like rich men that take pleasure
In hiding, more than handling, treasure.

By absence this good means I gain,
That I can catch her
Where none can watch her,
In some close corner of my brain.
There I embrace and kiss her,
And so I both enjoy and miss her.

**John Hoskins (1566–1638)**

# If you have lost everything but the love of your life:

## Sonnet 29

When, in disgrace with Fortune and men's eyes,
I all alone beweep my outcast state,
And trouble deaf heaven with my bootless cries,
And look upon myself and curse my fate,
Wishing me like to one more rich in hope,
Featured like him, like him with friends possessed,
Desiring this man's art, and that man's scope,
With what I most enjoy contented least,
Yet in these thoughts myself almost despising,
Haply I think on thee, and then my state,
Like to the lark at break of day arising
From sullen earth, sings hymns at heaven's gate;
For thy sweet love remembered such wealth brings,
That then I scorn to change my state with kings.

**William Shakespeare (1564–1616)**

# If you are tempted to a bigamous marriage:

## *from* The Beggar's Opera

One Wife is too much for most Husbands to hear,
But two at a time there's no mortal can bear.
This way, and that way, and which way I will,
What would comfort the one,
t' other Wife would take ill.

**John Gay (1685–1732)**

**If you and your partner have argued and you fear it's The End:**

# The Quarrel

Our quarrel seemed a giant thing,
It made the room feel mean and small,
The books, the lamp, the furniture,
The very pictures on the wall –

Crowded upon us as we sat
Pale and terrified, face to face.
'Why do you stay?' she said, 'my room
Can never be your resting place.'

'Katinka, ere we part for life,
I pray you walk once more with me.'
So down the dark, familiar road
We paced together, silently.

The sky – it seemed on fire with stars!
I said: – 'Katinka dear, look up!'
Like thirsty children, both of us
Drank from the giant loving cup.

'Who were those dolls?' Katinka said
'What were their stupid, vague alarms?'
And suddenly we turned and laughed
And rushed into each other's arms.

**Katherine Mansfield (1888–1923)**

## If you wonder why love seems to make no sense:

## Love, a Child, is Ever Crying

Love, a child, is ever crying;
Please him, and he straight is flying;
Give him, he the more is craving,
Never satisfied with having.

His desires have no measure;
Endless folly is his treasure;
What he promiseth he breaketh;
Trust not one word that he speaketh.

He vows nothing but false matter;
And to cozen you will flatter;
Let him gain the hand, he'll leave you
And still glory to deceive you.

He will triumph in your wailing;
And yet cause be of your failing:
These his virtues are, and slighter
Are his gifts, his favours lighter.

**If things turn really sour and you need some sound advice:**

## Marriage a-la-Mode

Why should a foolish marriage vow,
Which long ago was made,
Oblige us to each other now
When passion is decay'd?
We lov'd, and we lov'd, as long as we could,
Till our love was lov'd out in us both:
But our marriage is dead, when the pleasure is fled:
'Twas pleasure first made it an oath.

If I have pleasures for a friend,
And farther love in store,
What wrong has he whose joys did end,
And who could give no more?
'Tis a madness that he should be jealous of me,
Or that I should bar him of another:
For all we can gain is to give ourselves pain,
When neither can hinder the other.

**John Dryden (1631–1700)**

**If you grieve for one you love:**

# For Katrina's Sun Dial

Time is too slow for those who wait,
Too swift for those who fear,
Too long for those who grieve,
Too short for those who rejoice,
But for those who love, time is
Eternity.

**Henry van Dyke (1852–1933)**

# PARENTING

**If you are overwhelmed with parenting advice and just want some simple tips:**

## A Few Rules for Beginners

Babies must not eat the coal
And they must not make grimaces,
Nor in party dresses roll
And must never black their faces.

They must learn that pointing's rude,
They must sit quite still at table,
And must always eat the food
Put before them – if they're able.

If they fall, they must not cry,
Though it's known how painful this is;
No – there's always Mother by
Who will comfort them with kisses.

**Katherine Mansfield (1888–1923)**

## If you are concerned about your new baby's future prospects:

## On the Birth of his Son

Families, when a child is born
Want it to be intelligent.
I, through intelligence,
Having wrecked my whole life,
Only hope the baby will prove
Ignorant and stupid.
Then he will crown a tranquil life
By becoming a Cabinet Minister.

**Su Shi (1037–1101)**

**If your small child is taking your attention away from – well, everything:**

### *from* A Parental Ode to My Son, Aged Three Years and Five Months.

Thou happy, happy elf!
(But stop, – first let me kiss away that tear) –
Thou tiny image of myself!
(My love, he's poking peas into his ear!)
Thou merry, laughing sprite!
With spirits feather-light,
Untouch'd by sorrow, and unsoil'd by sin –
(Good heav'ns! the child is swallowing a pin!)

[...]

Thou little tricksy Puck!
With antic toys so funnily bestuck,
Light as the singing bird that wings the air –
(The door! the door! He'll tumble down the stair!)
Thou darling of thy sire!
(Why, Jane, he'll set his pinafore a-fire!)

Thou imp of mirth and joy!
In Love's dear chain so strong and bright a link,
Thou idol of thy parents – (Drat the boy!
There goes my ink!)

Thou pretty opening rose!
(Go to your mother, child, and wipe your nose!)
Balmy and breathing music like the South,
(He really brings my heart into my mouth!)
Fresh as the morn, and brilliant as its star, –
(I wish that window had an iron bar!)
Bold as the hawk, yet gentle as the dove, –
(I'll tell you what, my love,
I cannot write, unless he's sent above!)

**Thomas Hood (1799–1845)**

## If bath time with a toddler is not always joy unconfined:

# Washing and Dressing

Ah! why will my dear little girl be so cross,
And cry, and look sulky and pout?
To lose her sweet smile is a terrible loss,
I can't even kiss her without.

You say you don't like to be wash'd and be dress'd
But would you not wish to be clean?
Come, drive that long sob from your dear little breast,
This face is not fit to be seen.

If the water is cold, and the comb hurts your head,
And the soap has got into your eye,
Will the water grow warmer for all that you've said?
And what good will it do you to cry?

It is not to tease you, and hurt you, my sweet,
But only for kindness and care,
That I wash you and dress you, and make you look neat,
And comb out your tanglesome hair.

I don't mind the trouble, if you would not cry,
But pay me for all with a kiss;
That's right, take the towel and wipe your wet eye;
I thought you'd be good after this.

**Ann Taylor (1782–1866)**

**If the joy of raising a toddler sometimes loses its sparkle:**

# Characteristics of a Child Three Years Old

Loving she is, and tractable, though wild;
And Innocence hath privilege in her
To dignify arch looks and laughing eyes;
And feats of cunning; and the pretty round
Of trespasses, affected to provoke
Mock-chastisement and partnership in play.
And, as a faggot sparkles on the hearth,
Not less if unattended and alone
Than when both young and old sit gathered round
And take delight in its activity;
Even so this happy Creature of herself
Is all-sufficient, solitude to her
Is blithe society, who fills the air
With gladness and involuntary songs.

Light are her sallies as the tripping fawn's
Forth-startled from the fern where she lay couched;
Unthought-of, unexpected, as the stir
Of the soft breeze ruffling the meadow-flowers,
Or from before it chasing wantonly
The many-coloured images imprest
Upon the bosom of a placid lake.

**William Wordsworth (1770–1850)**

## If being a mother sometimes feels like the most thankless task in the world:

## Motherhood

The bravest battle that ever was fought!
Shall I tell you where and when?
On the maps of the world you will find it not;
'Twas fought by the mothers of men.

Nay not with the cannon of battle-shot,
With a sword or noble pen;
Nay, not with eloquent words or thought
From mouth of wonderful men!

But deep in a walled-up woman's heart –
Of a woman that would not yield,
But bravely, silently bore her part –
Lo, there is the battlefield!

No marshalling troops, no bivouac song,
No banner to gleam and wave;
But oh! those battles, they last so long –
From babyhood to the grave.

Yet, faithful still as a bridge of stars,
She fights in her walled-up town –
Fights on and on in her endless wars,
Then silent, unseen, goes down.

Oh, ye with banners and battle-shot,
And soldiers to shout and praise!
I tell you the kingliest victories fought
Were fought in those silent ways.

O spotless woman in a world of shame,
With splendid and silent scorn,
Go back to God as white as you came –
The Kingliest warrior born!

**Joaquin Miller (1837–1913)**

# If you spend a lot of time with a small but noisy child:

# De Puero Balbutiente
# (On a Child Learning to Speak)

Methinks 'tis pretty sport to hear a child
Rocking a word in mouth yet undefiled;
The tender racquet rudely plays the sound
Which, weakly bandied, cannot back rebound;
And the soft air, the softer roof doth kiss
With a sweet dying and a pretty miss,
Which hears no answer yet from the white rank
Of teeth not risen from their coral bank.
The alphabet is searched for letters soft
To try a word before it can be wrought;
And when it slideth forth, it goes as nice
As when a man doth walk upon the ice.

**Thomas Bastard (1566–1618)**

# FAMILY LIFE

## If you want to finally find out who walked that mud through the house:

## Mr Nobody

I know a funny little man,
As quiet as a mouse,
Who does the mischief that is done
In everybody's house!
There's no one ever sees his face,
And yet we all agree
That every plate we break was cracked
By Mr Nobody.

'Tis he who always tears out books,
Who leaves the door ajar,
He pulls the buttons from our shirts,
And scatters pins afar;
That squeaking door will always squeak,
For prithee, don't you see,
We leave the oiling to be done
By Mr Nobody.

He puts damp wood upon the fire,
That kettles cannot boil;
His are the feet that bring in mud,
And all the carpets soil.
The papers always are mislaid,
Who had them last but he?
There's not one tosses them about
But Mr Nobody.

The finger marks upon the door
By none of us are made;
We never leave the blinds unclosed,
To let the curtains fade.
The ink we never spill; the boots
That lying round you see
Are not our boots, – they all belong
To Mr Nobody.

**Anonymous**

## If you worry that nobody else's family is as strange as yours:

## On an Unsociable Family

O what a strange parcel of creatures are we,
Scarce ever to quarrel, or even agree;
We all are alone, though at home altogether,
Except to the fire constrained by the weather;
Then one says, 'Tis cold', which we all of us know,
And with unanimity answer, 'Tis so';
With shrugs and with shivers all look at the fire,
And shuffle ourselves and our chairs a bit nigher;
Then quickly, preceded by silence profound,
A yawn epidemical catches around:
Like social companions we never fall out,
Nor ever care what one another's about;
To comfort each other is never our plan,
For to please ourselves, truly, is more than we can.

**Elizabeth Hands (1746–1815)**

**If you worry that your home decor is not sophisticated enough:**

## A Home Song

I read within a poet's book
A word that starred the page:
'Stone walls do not a prison make,
Nor iron bars a cage!'

Yes, that is true; and something more
You'll find, where'er you roam,
That marble floors and gilded walls
Can never make a home.

But every house where Love abides,
And Friendship is a guest,
Is surely home, and home-sweet-home:
For there the heart can rest.

**Henry van Dyke (1852–1933)**

# If the endless round of housework is driving you crazy:

# A Tired Woman's Epitaph

Here lies a poor woman who was always tired.
She lived in a house where no help was hired.
Her last words on earth were, 'Dear friends I am going,
Where washing ain't done, nor sweeping or sewing.
But everything is exact to my wishes,
For where they don't eat, there will be no washing of dishes.
I will be where loud anthems will always be ringing,
But having no voice, I'll be clear of the singing, don't
mourn for me now, don't mourn for me never,
I'm going to do nothing, for ever and ever!'

**Anonymous**

**If you wonder what is going on inside the sleeping head on the pillow next to yours:**

## Dreams

Here we are all, by day; by night we're hurled
By dreams, each one, into a several world.

**Robert Herrick (1591–1674)**

## If it is your habit not to lock the bathroom door while bathing:

## The Bath

Broad is the Gate and wide the Path
That leads man to his daily bath;
But ere you spend the shining hour
With plunge and spray, with sluice and show'r –
With all that teaches you to dread
The bath as little as your bed –
Remember, whosoe'er you be,
To shut the door and turn the key!

I had a friend – my friend no more! –
Who failed to bolt his bath-room door;
A maiden aunt of his, one day,
Walked in, as half-submerged he lay!
She did not notice nephew John,
And turned the boiling water on!
He had no time, nor even scope
To camouflage himself with soap,

But gave a yell and flung aside
The sponge, 'neath which he sought to hide!
It fell to earth I know not where!
He beat his breast in his despair,
And then, like Venus from the foam,
Sprang into view, and made for home!
His aunt fell fainting to the ground!
Alas! They never brought her round!
She died, intestate, in her prime,
The victim of another's crime;
And John can never quite forget
How, by a breach of etiquette,
He lost, at one fell swoop (or plunge)
His aunt, his honour, and his sponge!

**Harry Graham (1874–1936)**

# LIFE'S
# TEMPTATIONS

**If you are always hungry for the latest new gadget:**

# Nature

As a fond mother, when the day is o'er,
Leads by the hand her little child to bed,
Half willing, half reluctant to be led,
And leave his broken playthings on the floor,
Still gazing at them through the open door,
Nor wholly reassured and comforted
By promises of others in their stead,
Which, though more splendid,
may not please him more;
So Nature deals with us, and takes away
Our playthings one by one, and by the hand
Leads us to rest so gently, that we go
Scarce knowing if we wish to go or stay,
Being too full of sleep to understand
How far the unknown transcends the what we know.

**Henry Wadsworth Longfellow (1807–1882)**

# If you are trying to give up smoking:

## *from* A Farewell to Tobacco

May the Babylonish curse,
Strait confound my stammering verse,
If I can a passage see
In this word-perplexity,
Or a fit expression find,
Or a language to my mind,
(Still the phrase is wide or scant)
To take leave of thee, GREAT PLANT!
Or in any terms relate
Half my love, or half my hate:
For I hate, yet love, thee so,
That, whichever thing I shew,
The plain truth will seem to be
A constrained hyperbole,
And the passion to proceed
More from a mistress than a weed.
[...]
For I must (nor let it grieve thee,
Friendliest of plants, that I must) leave thee.

**Charles Lamb (1775–1834)**

**If you are criticised for having a quiet pint instead of doing something 'more useful':**

# Beer

Here,
With my beer
I sit,
While golden moments flit:
Alas!
They pass
Unheeded by:
And, as they fly,
I,
Being dry,
Sit, idly sipping here
My beer.

O, finer far
Than fame, or riches, are
The graceful smoke-wreaths of this free cigar!
Why
Should I
Weep, wail, or sigh?

What if luck has passed me by?
What if my hopes are dead, –
My pleasures fled?
Have I not still
My fill
Of right good cheer, –
Cigars and beer?

Go, whining youth,
Forsooth!
Go, weep and wail,
Sigh and grow pale,
Weave melancholy rhymes
On the old times,
Whose joys like shadowy ghosts appear,
But leave me to my beer!
Gold is dross,
Love is loss,
So, if I gulp my sorrows down,
Or see them drown
In foamy draughts of old nut-brown,
Then do I wear the crown,
Without the cross!

**George Arnold (1834–1865)**

# If you are considering giving up alcohol to achieve a longer life:

## The Horse and Mule

The horse and mule live thirty years
And nothing know of wines and beers;
The goat and sheep at twenty die
And never taste of Scotch or Rye;
The cow drinks water by the ton
And at eighteen is mostly done;
The dog at fifteen cashes in
And without the aid of rum or gin;
The cat in milk and water soaks
And then in twelve short years it croaks;
The modest, sober, bone-dry hen
Lays eggs for nogs, then dies at ten.
All animals are strictly dry,
They sinless live and early die.
But sinful, ginful, rum-soaked men –
Survive for three-score years and ten!
And some of us... though mighty few
Stay pickled 'til we're ninety-two.

**Anonymous**

**If a 'healthy diet' sounds dreary and you need some inspiration:**

## A Recipe for Salad

To make this condiment your poet begs
The pounded yellow of two hard boiled eggs;
Two boiled potatoes, passed through kitchen sieve,
Smoothness and softness to the salad give;
Let onion atoms lurk within the bowl,
And, half suspected, animate the whole;
Of mordant mustard add a single spoon,
Distrust the condiment that bites so soon;
But deem it not, thou man of herbs, a fault
To add a double quantity of salt;
Four times the spoon with oil from Lucca crown,
And twice with vinegar, procured from town;
And lastly, o'er the flavoured compound toss
A magic soupçon of anchovy sauce.
O green and glorious! O herbaceous treat!
'T would tempt the dying anchorite to eat;
Back to the world he'd turn his fleeting soul,
And plunge his fingers in the salad-bowl!
Serenely full, the epicure would say,
'Fate cannot harm me, – I have dined to-day.'

**Sydney Smith (1771–1845)**

# WORK AND MONEY

# If you are trying to balance work and life:

## *from* Linden Lea

Within the woodlands, flow'ry gladed,
By the oak trees' mossy moot,
The shining grass blades, timber-shaded,
Now do quiver underfoot;
And birds do whistle overhead,
And water's bubbling in its bed,
And there, for me, the apple tree
Do lean down low in Linden Lea.

[...]

Let other folk make money faster
In the air of dark-roomed towns,
I don't dread a peevish master;
Though no man do heed my frowns,
I be free to go abroad,
Or take again my homeward road
To where, for me, the apple tree
Do lean down low in Linden Lea.

**William Barnes (1801–1886)**

**If you are spending too much of your life in a dark and airless office:**

## The World Is Too Much With Us

The world is too much with us; late and soon,
Getting and spending, we lay waste our powers;
Little we see in Nature that is ours;
We have given our hearts away, a sordid boon!
This Sea that bares her bosom to the moon,
The winds that will be howling at all hours,
And are up-gathered now like sleeping flowers,
For this, for everything, we are out of tune;
It moves us not. – Great God! I'd rather be
A Pagan suckled in a creed outworn;
So might I, standing on this pleasant lea,
Have glimpses that would make me less forlorn;
Have sight of Proteus rising from the sea;
Or hear old Triton blow his wreathèd horn.

**William Wordsworth (1770–1850)**

**If your colleagues invite you out for a drink on a 'school night':**

## *from* Let's Be Fools To-Night, or The Three Partners

We, three men of commerce,
Men of business we,
Gave but little promise
Of ability
When we lived in riot;
Never drew the line,
Hating peace and quiet,
Loving maids and wine.

Days when money goes, days
When men's hearts are right;
We were fools in those days,
Let's be fools to-night.

We must wear to-morrow
All our worldly marks,
Calm looks for our sorrow,
Stern looks for our clerks,
Who, from trouble shrinking,
Tasting earthly joys,
Hate us, little thinking
Ever we were boys.

Days when kindness flows, days
When men's hearts are white;
We've been wise since those days,
Let's be fools to-night.

**Henry Lawson (1867–1922)**

## If you are criticised for choosing not to race up the career ladder:

# *from* Upon a Snail

She goes but softly, but she goeth sure,
She stumbles not, as stronger creatures do;
Her journey's shorter, so she may endure
Better than they which do much further go.

She makes no noise, but stilly seizeth on
The flower or herb appointed for her food;
The which she quietly doth feed upon,
While others range and glare, but find no good.

And though she doth but very softly go,
However slow her pace be, yet 'tis sure;
And certainly they that do travel so,
The prize which they do aim at they procure.

**John Bunyan (1628–1688)**

# If you are tempted to participate in a dodgy deal:

## The Honest Dealer

All of us know that money talks
throughout our glorious nation;
But money whispers low compared to
business reputations;
Pull off no slick nor crooked deal,
for pennies or for dollars.
God! Think of all the trade you'll lose
if just one sucker hollers!

**Anonymous**

# If your wallet is unaccountably empty (again):

# *from* The Complaint of Chaucer to his Purse

To you, my purse, and to none other wight
    Complain I, for you be my lady dear!
I am so sorry, now that you be light;
For certain, but you make me heavy cheer,
Me were as lief be laid upon my bier;
    For which unto your mercy thus I cry:
    Be heavy again, or else might I die!

Now voucheth safe this day, or be it night,
That I of you the blissful sound may hear,
Or see your colour like the sun bright,
    That of yellowness had never peer.
You be my life, you be mine heart's steer,
    Queen of comfort and of good company:
    Be heavy again, or else might I die!

Now, purse, that be to me my life's light
And saviour, as done in this world here,
Out of this town help me through your might,
Since that you will not be my treasurer;
For I am shaved as nigh as any friar.
But yet I pray unto your courtesy:
Be heavy again, or else might I die!

**Geoffrey Chaucer (*c.*1343–1400)**

# If you have a happy life but wish you were richer:

## Sweet Content

Art thou poor, yet hast thou golden slumbers?
O sweet content!
Art thou rich, yet is thy mind perplex'd?
O punishment!
Dost thou laugh to see how fools are vex'd
To add to golden numbers golden numbers?
O sweet content! O sweet, O sweet content!
Work apace, apace, apace, apace;
Honest labour bears a lovely face;
Then hey nonny nonny – hey nonny nonny!

Canst drink the waters of the crispèd spring?
O sweet content!
Swim'st thou in wealth, yet sink'st in thine own tears?
O punishment!
Then he that patiently want's burden bears,
No burden bears, but is a king, a king!
O sweet content! O sweet, O sweet content!
Work apace, apace, apace, apace;
Honest labour bears a lovely face;
Then hey nonny nonny – hey nonny nonny!

**Thomas Dekker (1572–1632)**

# If you want to know how to be rich:

## How to get RICHES

In Things of moment, on thy self depend,
Nor trust too far thy Servant or thy Friend:
With private Views, thy Friend may promise fair,
And Servants very seldom prove sincere.

What can be done, with Care perform to day,
Dangers unthought-of will attend Delay;
Your distant Prospects all precarious are,
And Fortune is as fickle as she's fair.

Nor trivial Loss, nor trivial Gain despise;
Molehills, if often heap'd, to Mountains rise:
Weigh every small Expence, and nothing waste,
Farthings long sav'd amount to Pounds at last.

**Benjamin Franklin (1706–1790)**

# If being gentle and polite has failed to get you where you want to be in life:

## Ambition

Get place and wealth; if possible, with grace;
If not, by any means get wealth and place.

**Alexander Pope (1688–1744)**

# If you are jealous of somebody else's wealth:

# *from* The Vanities of Life

What are life's joys and gains?
What pleasures crowd its ways,
That man should take such pains
To seek them all his days?
Sift this untoward strife
On which thy mind is bent:
See if this chaff of life
Is worth the trouble spent.

[...]

Whoso with riches deals,
And thinks peace bought and sold,
Will find them slipping eels,
That slide the firmest hold:
Though sweet as sleep with health
Thy lulling luck may be,
Pride may oerstride thy wealth,
And check prosperity.

**John Clare (1793–1864)**

# DEALING WITH PEOPLE

**If you are annoyed because somebody else has just told your best joke:**

## Wisdom and Folly

Fools make feasts and wise men eat them;
Wise men make jests and fools repeat them.

**Anonymous**

**If you don't know whether it's best to be serious or to make people laugh:**

## III Mon. May hath xxxi days.

Mirth pleaseth some, to others 'tis offence,
Some commend plain conceit, some profound sense;
Some wish a witty Jest, some dislike that,
And most would have themselves they know not what.
Then he that would please all, and himself too,
Takes more in hand than he is like to do.

**Benjamin Franklin (1706–1790)**

## If you are on the receiving end of snobbery:

# A Prouder Man Than You

If you fancy that your people came of better
stock than mine,
If you hint of higher breeding by a word or by a sign,
If you're proud because of fortune or the
clever things you do,
Then I'll play no second fiddle:
I'm a prouder man than you!

If you think that your profession has the more gentility,
And that you are condescending to be seen
along with me;
If you notice that I'm shabby while your clothes
are spruce and new,
You have only got to hint it:
I'm a prouder man than you!

If you have a swell companion when you see
me on the street,
And you think that I'm too common for your
toney friend to meet,

So that I, in passing closely, fail to come
within your view,
Then be blind to me for ever:
I'm a prouder man than you!

If your character be blameless,
if your outward past be clean,
While 'tis known my antecedents are
not what they should have been,
Do not risk contamination,
save your name whate'er you do,
`Birds o' feather fly together':
I'm a prouder bird than you!

Keep your patronage for others!
Gold and station cannot hide
Friendship that can laugh at fortune,
friendship that can conquer pride!
Offer this as to an equal, let me see that you are true,
And my wall of pride is shattered:
I am not so proud as you!

**Henry Lawson (1867–1922)**

# If you are angry with someone:

# *from* Think Gently of the Erring

Think gently of the erring:
Ye know not of the power
With which the dark temptation came
In some unguarded hour.
Ye may not know how earnestly
They struggled, or how well,
Until the hour of weakness came
And sadly thus they fell.

[...]

Speak gently to the erring:
For is it not enough
That innocence and peace have gone,
Without thy censure rough?
It sure must be a weary lot,
That sin-stained heart to bear,
And those who share a happier fate
Their chidings well may spare.

**Julia Carney (1823–1908)**

**If your soul has been worn thin by a long evening of small-talk:**

## *from* Gnosis

What is social company
But a babbling summer stream?
What our wise philosophy
But the glancing of a dream?

Only when the Sun of Love
Melts the scattered stars of thought,
Only when we live above
What the dim-eyed world hath taught,

Only when our souls are fed
By the Fount which gave them birth,
And by inspiration led
Which they never drew from earth,

We, like parted drops of rain,
Swelling till they meet and run,
Shall all be absorbed again,
Melting, flowing, into one.

**Christopher Pearse Cranch (1813–1892)**

**If you worry about feeling jealous of a friend's success:**

## *from* Verses on the Death of Dr Swift, D.S.P.D.

We all behold with envious Eyes,
Our Equal rais'd above our Size;
Who wou'd not at a crowded Show,
Stand high himself, keep others low?
I love my Friend as well as you,
But would not have him stop my View;
Then let him have the higher Post;
I ask but for an Inch at most.

If in a Battle you should find,
One, whom you love of all Mankind,
Had some heroick Action done,
A Champion kill'd, or Trophy won;
Rather than thus be over-topt,
Would you not wish his Lawrels cropt?

Dear honest Ned is in the Gout,
Lies rackt with Pain, and you without:
How patiently you hear him groan!
How glad the Case is not your own!

What Poet would not grieve to see,
His Brethren write as well as he?
But rather than they should excel,
He'd wish his Rivals all in Hell.

Her End when Emulation misses,
She turns to Envy, Stings and Hisses:
The strongest Friendship yields to Pride,
Unless the Odds be on our Side.

[...]

To all my Foes, dear Fortune, send
Thy Gifts, but never to my Friend:
I tamely can endure the first,
But, this with Envy makes me burst.

**Jonathan Swift (1667–1745)**

# ON HEALTH
# AND
# EMOTIONS

**If you feel that no one on earth understands
what your toothache feels like:**

## Address to the Toothache

My curse upon your venom'd stang,
That shoots my tortur'd gums alang,
An' thro' my lug gies mony a twang,
Wi' gnawing vengeance,
Tearing my nerves wi' bitter pang,
Like racking engines!

When fevers burn, or argues freezes,
Rheumatics gnaw, or colics squeezes,
Our neibor's sympathy can ease us,
Wi' pitying moan;
But thee – thou hell o' a' diseases –
They mock our groan.

Adown my beard the slavers trickle
I throw the wee stools o'er the mickle,
While round the fire the giglets keckle,
To see me loup,
While, raving mad, I wish a heckle
Were in their doup!

In a' the numerous human dools,
Ill hairsts, daft bargains, cutty stools,
Or worthy frien's rak'd i' the mools, –
    Sad sight to see!
The tricks o' knaves, or fash o'fools,
    Thou bear'st the gree!

Where'er that place be priests ca' hell,
Where a' the tones o' misery yell,
An' ranked plagues their numbers tell,
    In dreadfu' raw,
Thou, toothache, surely bear'st the bell,
    Amang them a'!

O thou grim, mischief-making chiel,
That gars the notes o' discord squeel,
Till daft mankind aft dance a reel
    In gore, a shoe-thick,
Gie a' the faes o' Scotland's weal
    A townmond's toothache!

**Robert Burns (1759–1796)**

**If you are ill in bed:**

# In the Hospital

Because on the branch that is tapping my pane
A sun-wakened leaf-bud, uncurled,
Is bursting its rusty brown sheathing in twain,
I know there is Spring in the world.

Because through the sky-patch whose azure and white
My window frames all the day long,
A yellow-bird dips for an instant of flight,
I know there is Song.

Because even here in this Mansion of Woe
Where creep the dull hours, leaden-shod,
Compassion and Tenderness aid me, I know
There is God.

**Arthur Guiterman (1871–1943)**

# If you are so sad that you feel you will never smile again:

## *from* Joy and Sorrow

Then a woman said, 'Speak to us of Joy and Sorrow.'
And he answered:
Your joy is your sorrow unmasked.
And the selfsame well from which your laughter rises
was oftentimes filled with your tears.
And how else can it be?
The deeper that sorrow carves into your being, the
more joy you can contain.
Is not the cup that holds your wine the very cup that
was burned in the potter's oven?
And is not the lute that soothes your spirit, the very
wood that was hollowed with knives?
When you are joyous, look deep into your heart and
you shall find it is only that which has given you
sorrow that is giving you joy.
When you are sorrowful look again in your heart, and
you shall see that in truth you are weeping for that
which has been your delight.

**Kahlil Gibran (1883–1931)**

**If life feels pointless and you'd rather just stay indoors by yourself:**

# If I Can Stop One Heart from Breaking

If I can stop one heart from breaking,
I shall not live in vain;
If I can ease one life the aching,
Or cool one pain,
Or help one fainting robin
Unto his nest again,
I shall not live in vain.

**Emily Dickinson (1830–1886)**

## If you long for a fresh start:

# New Every Morning

Every day is a fresh beginning,
Listen my soul to the glad refrain.
And, spite of old sorrows
And older sinning,
Troubles forecasted
And possible pain,
Take heart with the day and begin again.

**Susan Coolidge (1835–1905)**

# AGEING
# (DIS)GRACEFULLY

## If you are tired of being told to act your age:

# Father William

'You are old, Father William,' the young man said,
　'And your hair has become very white;
And yet you incessantly stand on your head –
　Do you think, at your age, it is right?'

'In my youth,' Father William replied to his son,
　'I feared it would injure the brain;
But now that I'm perfectly sure I have none,
　Why, I do it again and again.'

'You are old,' said the youth, 'as I mentioned before,
　And have grown most uncommonly fat;
Yet you turned a back-somersault in at the door –
　Pray, what is the reason of that?'

'In my youth,' said the sage, as he shook his grey locks,
　'I kept all my limbs very supple
By the use of this ointment – one shilling the box –
　Allow me to sell you a couple.'

'You are old,' said the youth, 'and your jaws are too weak
For anything tougher than suet;
Yet you finished the goose, with the bones and the beak –
Pray, how did you manage to do it?'

'In my youth,' said his father, 'I took to the law,
And argued each case with my wife;
And the muscular strength, which it gave to my jaw,
Has lasted the rest of my life.'

'You are old,' said the youth; 'one would hardly suppose
That your eye was as steady as ever;
Yet you balanced an eel on the end of your nose –
What made you so awfully clever?'

'I have answered three questions, and that is enough,'
Said his father; 'don't give yourself airs!
Do you think I can listen all day to such stuff?
Be off, or I'll kick you down stairs!'

**Lewis Carroll (1832–1898)**

## If you are accused of acting oddly in your old age:

## Why Should Not Old Men Be Mad?

Why should not old men be mad?
Some have known a likely lad
That had a sound fly-fisher's wrist
Turn to a drunken journalist;
A girl that knew all Dante once
Live to bear children to a dunce;
A Helen of social welfare dream,
Climb on a wagonette to scream.
Some think it a matter of course that chance
Should starve good men and bad advance,
That if their neighbours figured plain,
As though upon a lighted screen,
No single story would they find
Of an unbroken happy mind,
A finish worthy of the start.

Young men know nothing of this sort,
Observant old men know it well;
And when they know what old books tell
And that no better can be had,
Know why an old man should be mad.

**William Butler Yeats (1865–1939)**

**If you are obsessed with finding an anti-ageing cream that actually works:**

# The True Beauty

He that loves a rosy cheek,
Or a coral lip admires,
Or from star-like eyes doth seek
Fuel to maintain his fires;
As old Time makes these decay,
So his flames must waste away.

But a smooth and steadfast mind,
Gentle thoughts, and calm desires,
Hearts with equal love combined,
Kindle never-dying fires:
Where these are not, I despise
Lovely cheeks or lips or eyes.

**Thomas Carew (1595–1640)**

**If an old friend is distressed about his greying hair:**

# *from* John Anderson, My Jo

John Anderson, my jo, John,
When we were first acquent;
Your locks were like the raven,
Your bonie brow was brent;
But now your brow is beld, John,
Your locks are like the snaw;
But blessings on your frosty pow,
John Anderson, my jo.

**Robert Burns (1759–1796)**

**If you worry about the age difference between you and your partner:**

## To Chloe: Who for His Sake Wished Herself Younger

There are two births; the one when light
First strikes the new awaken'd sense;
The other when two souls unite,
And we must count our life from thence:
When you loved me and I loved you
Then both of us were born anew.

Love then to us new souls did give
And in those souls did plant new powers;
Since when another life we live,
The breath we breathe is his, not ours:
Love makes those young whom age doth chill,
And whom he finds young keeps young still.

**William Cartwright (1611–1643)**

**If you dream of a retirement idyll:**

# The Lake Isle of Innisfree

I will arise and go now, and go to Innisfree,
And a small cabin build there,
of clay and wattles made;
Nine bean rows will I have there,
a hive for the honey bee,
And live alone in the bee-loud glade.

And I shall have some peace there,
for peace comes dropping slow,
Dropping from the veils of the morning to
where the cricket sings;
There midnight's all a glimmer,
and noon a purple glow,
And evening full of the linnet's wings.

I will arise and go now, for always night and day
I hear lake water lapping with low
sounds by the shore;
While I stand on the roadway or
on the pavements gray,
I hear it in the deep heart's core.

**William Butler Yeats (1865–1939)**

# LIFE'S BIG
# QUESTIONS

## If you find it hard to put your dreams and plans into action:

## *from* A Psalm of Life

Lives of great men all remind us
We can make our lives sublime,
And, departing, leave behind us
Footprints on the sands of time;

Footprints, that perhaps another,
Sailing o'er life's solemn main,
A forlorn and shipwrecked brother,
Seeing, shall take heart again.

Let us, then, be up and doing,
With a heart for any fate;
Still achieving, still pursuing,
Learn to labor and to wait.

**Henry Wadsworth Longfellow (1807–1882)**

## If you need an antidote to procrastination:

## *from* Night Thoughts

Be wise to-day; 'tis madness to defer;
Next day the fatal precedent will plead;
Thus on, till wisdom is push'd out of life.
Procrastination is the thief of time;
Year after year it steals, till all are fled,
And to the mercies of a moment leaves
The vast concerns of an eternal scene.
If not so frequent, would not this be strange?
That 'tis so frequent, this is stranger still.

**Edward Young (1681–1765)**

# If you feel that your efforts are too tiny to make any difference to the world:

## *from* Little Things

Little drops of water,
Little grains of sand,
Make the mighty ocean
And the pleasant land.

Little deeds of kindness,
Little words of love,
Make our world an Eden
Like the Heaven above.

**Julia Carney (1823–1908)**

**If you feel that today is just another day:**

## To the Sun-Dial

Thou silent herald of Time's silent flight!
Say, could'st thou speak, what warning voice were thine?
Shade, who canst only show how others shine!
Dark, sullen witness of resplendent light
In day's broad glare, and when the moontide bright
Of laughing fortune sheds the ray divine,
Thy ready favors cheer us — but decline
The clouds of morning and the gloom of night.
Yet are thy counsels faithful, just, and wise;
They bid us seize the moments as they pass —
Snatch the retrieveless sunbeam as it flies,
Nor lose one sand of life's revolving glass —
Aspiring still, with energy sublime,
By virtuous deeds to give eternity to Time.

**John Quincy Adams (1767–1848)**

**If you wonder what's the best way
to live contentedly:**

# The Character of a Happy Life

How happy is he born and taught
That serveth not another's will;
Whose armour is his honest thought,
And simple truth his utmost skill!

Whose passions not his masters are;
Whose soul is still prepared for death,
Untied unto the world by care
Of public fame or private breath;

Who envies none that chance doth raise,
Nor vice; who never understood
How deepest wounds are given by praise;
Nor rules of state, but rules of good;

Who hath his life from rumours freed;
Whose conscience is his strong retreat;
Whose state can neither flatterers feed,
Nor ruin make oppressors great;

Who God doth late and early pray
More of His grace than gifts to lend;
And entertains the harmless day
With a religious book or friend;

– This man is freed from servile bands
Of hope to rise or fear to fall:
Lord of himself, though not of lands,
And having nothing, yet hath all.

**Sir Henry Wotton (1568–1639)**

# If you are looking for advice on how to lead your life:

# If –

If you can keep your head when all about you
Are losing theirs and blaming it on you,
If you can trust yourself when all men doubt you,
But make allowance for their doubting too;
If you can wait and not be tired by waiting,
Or being lied about, don't deal in lies,
Or being hated, don't give way to hating,
And yet don't look too good, nor talk too wise:

If you can dream – and not make dreams your master;
If you can think – and not make thoughts your aim;
If you can meet with Triumph and Disaster
And treat those two impostors just the same;
If you can bear to hear the truth you've spoken
Twisted by knaves to make a trap for fools,
Or watch the things you gave your life to, broken,
And stoop and build 'em up with worn-out tools:

If you can make one heap of all your winnings
And risk it on one turn of pitch-and-toss,
And lose, and start again at your beginnings
And never breathe a word about your loss;
If you can force your heart and nerve and sinew
To serve your turn long after they are gone,
And so hold on when there is nothing in you
Except the Will which says to them: 'Hold on!'

If you can talk with crowds and keep your virtue,
Or walk with Kings – nor lose the common touch,
If neither foes nor loving friends can hurt you,
If all men count with you, but none too much;
If you can fill the unforgiving minute
With sixty seconds' worth of distance run,
Yours is the Earth and everything that's in it,
And – which is more – you'll be a Man, my son!

**Rudyard Kipling (1865–1936)**

**If you wish you could say, 'I did it my way', but you need some encouragement:**

# Happy the Man
# (A Translation from Horace's Odes)

Happy the man, and happy he alone,
He who can call today his own:
He who, secure within, can say,
Tomorrow do thy worst, for I have lived today.
Be fair or foul or rain or shine
The joys I have possessed, in spite of fate, are mine.
Not Heaven itself upon the past has power,
But what has been, has been, and I have had my hour.

**John Dryden (1631–1700)**

# THROUGH
# THE YEAR

## If you feel that modern life is erasing the rhythm of the seasons:

# A Monthly Rune

January: By this fire I warm my hands,
February: And with my spade I delve my lands.
March: Here I set my seeds to spring,
April: And here I hear the birds to sing.
May: I am as light as bird in the treetop,
June: And I take pains to weed my crop.
July: With my scythe my mead I mow,
August: And here I shear my corn full low.
September: With my flail I earn my bread,
October: And here I sow my wheat so red.
November: At Martinmas I kill my swine,
December: And at Yule I drink red wine.

**Traditional**

## If New Year celebrations seem to be lacking a deeper meaning:

# *from* Ring Out, Wild Bells

Ring out, wild bells, to the wild sky,
The flying cloud, the frosty light;
The year is dying in the night;
Ring out, wild bells, and let him die.

Ring out the old, ring in the new,
Ring, happy bells, across the snow:
The year is going, let him go;
Ring out the false, ring in the true.

Ring out the grief that saps the mind,
For those that here we see no more,
Ring out the feud of rich and poor,
Ring in redress to all mankind.

Ring out a slowly dying cause,
And ancient forms of party strife;
Ring in the nobler modes of life,
With sweeter manners, purer laws.

**Alfred, Lord Tennyson (1809–1892)**

**If you fear that the gloom of February will never end:**

## Last Week of February, 1890

Hark to the merry birds, hark how they sing!
Although 'tis not yet spring
And keen the air;
Hale Winter, half resigning ere he go,
Doth to his heiress shew
His kingdom fair.

In patient russet is his forest spread,
All bright with bramble red,
With beechen moss
And holly sheen: the oak silver and stark
Sunneth his aged bark
And wrinkled boss.

But 'neath the ruin of the withered brake
Primroses now awake
From nursing shades:
The crumpled carpet of the dry leaves brown
Avails not to keep down
The hyacinth blades.

The hazel hath put forth his tassels ruffed;
The willow's flossy tuft
Hath slipped him free:
The rose amid her ransacked orange hips
Braggeth the tender tips
Of bowers to be.

A black rook stirs the branches here and there,
Foraging to repair
His broken home:
And hark, on the ash boughs! Never thrush did sing
Louder in praise of spring,
When spring is come.

**Robert Bridges (1844–1930)**

**If another rainy day leads you to forget how beautiful the countryside is:**

# Home Thoughts from Abroad

Oh, to be in England
Now that April's there,
And whoever wakes in England
Sees, some morning, unaware,
That the lowest boughs and the brushwood sheaf
Round the elm-tree bole are in tiny leaf,
While the chaffinch sings on the orchard bough
In England – now!
And after April, when May follows,
And the whitethroat builds, and all the swallows!
Hark, where my blossomed pear-tree in the hedge
Leans to the field and scatters on the clover
Blossoms and dewdrops – at the bent spray's edge -
That's the wise thrush; he sings each song twice over,

Lest you should think he never could recapture
The first fine careless rapture!
And though the fields look rough with hoary dew
All will be gay when noontide wakes anew
The buttercups, the little children's dower
– Far brighter than this gaudy melon-flower!

**Robert Browning (1812–1889)**

**If you're seeking a little cheer on a dreary day:**

## Ballade Made in the Hot Weather

Fountains that frisk and sprinkle
The moss they overspill;
Pools that the breezes crinkle;
The wheel beside the mill,
With its wet, weedy frill;
Wind-shadows in the wheat;
A water-cart in the street;
The fringe of foam that girds
An islet's ferneries;
A green sky's minor thirds –
To live, I think of these!

Of ice and glass the tinkle,
Pellucid, silver-shrill;
Peaches without a wrinkle;
Cherries and snow at will,
From china bowls that fill
The senses with a sweet
Incuriousness of heat;

A melon's dripping sherds;
Cream-clotted strawberries;
Dusk dairies set with curds –
To live, I think of these!

Vale-lily and periwinkle;
Wet stone-crop on the sill;
The look of leaves a-twinkle
With windlets clear and still;
The feel of a forest rill
That wimples fresh and fleet
About one's naked feet;
The muzzles of drinking herds;
Lush flags and bulrushes;
The chirp of rain-bound birds –
To live, I think of these!

*Envoy*

Dark aisles, new packs of cards,
Mermaidens' tails, cool swards,
Dawn dews and starlit seas,
White marbles, whiter words –
To live, I think of these!

**William Ernest Henley (1849–1903)**

**If you feel you're the only one who finds firework displays utterly tedious:**

## *from* The Palace

Others may praise the 'grand displays'
Where 'fiery arch', 'cascade' and 'comet,'
Set the whole garden in a 'blaze'!
Far, at such times, may I be from it;
Though then the public may be 'lost
In wonder' at a trifling cost.

Fann'd by the breeze, to puff at ease
My faithful pipe is all I crave:
And if folks rave about the 'trees
Lit up by fireworks', let them rave.
Your monster fetes, I like not these;
Though they bring grist to the lessees.

**Charles Stuart Calverley (1831–1884)**

# If you are cursing the raw, blustery winter weather:

# *from* Ode to the North-East Wind

Welcome, wild North-easter!
Shame it is to see
Odes to every zephyr;
Ne'er a verse to thee.
Welcome, black North-easter!
O'er the German foam;
O'er the Danish moorlands,
From thy frozen home.
Tired we are of summer,
Tired of gaudy glare,
Showers soft and steaming,
Hot and breathless air.
Tired of listless dreaming,
Through the lazy day:
Jovial wind of winter
Turn us out to play!

**Charles Kingsley (1819–1875)**

## If winter feels like a hopeless time of death and gloom:

## *from* Winter

I, singularly moved
To love the lovely that are not beloved,
Of all the Seasons, most
Love Winter, and to trace
The sense of the Trophonian pallor on her face.
It is not death, but plenitude of peace;
And the dim cloud that does the world enfold
Hath less the characters of dark and cold
Than warmth and light asleep,
And correspondent breathing seems to keep
With the infant harvest, breathing soft below
Its eider coverlet of snow.
Nor is in field or garden anything
But, duly look'd into, contains serene
The substance of things hoped for, in the Spring,
And evidence of Summer not yet seen.

**Coventry Patmore (1823–1896)**

**If you are vexed to find yet another band of carol singers at your door:**

## Minstrels

The minstrels played their Christmas tune
To-night beneath my cottage-eaves;
While, smitten by a lofty moon,
The encircling laurels, thick with leaves,
Gave back a rich and dazzling sheen,
That overpowered their natural green.

Through hill and valley every breeze
Had sunk to rest with folded wings:
Keen was the air, but could not freeze,
Nor check, the music of the strings;
So stout and hardy were the band
That scraped the chords with strenuous hand.

And who but listened? – till was paid
Respect to every inmate's claim,
The greeting given, the music played
In honour of each household name,
Duly pronounced with lusty call,
And 'Merry Christmas' wished to all.

**William Wordsworth (1770–1850)**

# INDEX OF POETS

Have you enjoyed this book?
If so, why not write a review on your favourite website?

If you're interested in finding out more about
our books, find us on Facebook at
**Summersdale Publishers** and follow us
on Twitter at **@Summersdale**.

Thanks very much for buying this Summersdale book.

# www.summersdale.com